How to be Heartbroken

E. P. Johnson

Dedicated to Kaitlin Washburn,
fearless journalist and my best friend

Table of Contents

Introduction

This book is the step-by-step process I went through to authentically feel my heartbreak and cope with my losses of love. I cover a two-year period of my life that changed the course of my emotional footprint. I hope that this book of overly dramatic poetry acts as a roadmap to self love, independence, and feeling your sad feelings.

I am excited to share with you my sad chapter with a happy boy.

You don't always realize how much of an impact someone make in your life until after it's over. And even further, you don't always give that person credit. So this book is dedicated to a sad place in my life when I met the love of my life. Not only did he pull me through but he taught me that I could be happy again. For this I am forever grateful.

Forget me not my forbidden love.

Step 1
Cry with no reason and do it often

Step 1: Cry with no reason and do it often

I looked into my life
And saw that you were the ribbon holding my happy memories
together
I saw the pain you had caused
And that I allowed you to be there
My happiest memories were tied up in you
But in my choosing to cut them loose
I liberate you
And I liberarte me

Goodbye my love
Be free

Step 1: Cry with no reason and do it often

Sometimes I cry
Remembering tears I shed
Discarded by you

Dear Self,

We have but one rule in this house about crying. You can only cry about a guy if you know his middle name. This is frivolous you may think, but quite contrary. If you knew his middle name, he was something special.

It means you probably knew his favorite color or that when you smiled it brightened his day. Or that he really missed his sister and that they had a close relationship. Or even that time that he called you "pure sex" and it made you laugh for an entire week but that type of laugh when your heart flutters.

You knew so much more than his middle name and maybe he's still not worth a single one of your tears. But you at least have a valid reason to be crying.

Please stop crying,
Self

Even a simple photo
of you
Reminds me of what we had

I am reminded that
I will never be happier
Than I was
When I was with
you

God how I miss you

Sometimes I pray
That you would hold me one more time

Our bodies fit together like puzzle pieces
But our lives never will

Step 1: Cry with no reason and do it often

When I want to give up on love
I first remember all the bad things you said
You said you never loved me
You said that in ten years you thought you would be dead
You once stopped talking to me for three days
You stopped wanting me to touch your hair
And then later you wanted me to stop touching you all together
But then I remember all the nice things you said
You once called me pure sex
You once laid beside me and looked at me and smiled and said that
I was so beautiful
You later cried and told me you didn't want to lose me when you
dumped me
All these things leave me all kinds of washed up
I don't know how to feel
About you
Or anyone

Step 1: Cry with no reason and do it often

Hey it's me,
I'm crying again.

These tears feel so useless
This pain feels so unnecessary
But it feels better than the fog
Feeling always feels better than nothing
I would rather writhe in pain for the rest of my life
Than be a numb entity
This sadness that I feel is all consuming
But apathy bites

Step 1: Cry with no reason and do it often

It is just as important to feel your emotions leave
As it is to feel them enter
But what if the bad ones never leave
What if this never leaves me?
What if my heartbreak never heals?
What if my blue heart never loves again?

Step 1: Cry with no reason and do it often

I'm ready to just love
And that be it
I'm ready to never find love again
Maybe I'll get married
Maybe I'll be a spinster
I might even love again
But I don't think I'll ever fall in love again
You were the one
You were it
I am so in love with you
And it will only ever be that

Step 1: Cry with no reason and do it often

I'm sad today
That's a normal, everyday emotion
That's something I have the right to feel without anyone feeling the
need to change my state of mind
Let me be sad
Let me cry
Don't tell me how to walk around sadness
Let me walk through it
And if you want to support me
Be there on the other side

Step 1: Cry with no reason and do it often

Hey there depression
You're making your rounds again
Why can't you leave me so I can focus
I hardly feel motivated to do anything
I don't want to work
I don't want to eat
I don't want to sleep
I don't even want to breathe
You take every last drop from my cup
And turn me away from the only One who can fill it
Thanks for that

Step 1: Cry with no reason and do it often

If I think hard enough I can feel you kissing my neck
Like a phantom of the experience we shared
The ghost of our love eludes me
Whispering the same sweet nothing's of hope in my ears
That fleeting feeling
Enchants me

Step 1: Cry with no reason and do it often

Every time you become a distant memory
And I feel as though it might finally pass
I might finally forget
I fall in love with you again

You will always be the love of my life.

Step 1: Cry with no reason and do it often

It's not about the one you can live with
It's all about the one you can't live without
And I can't live without you
But I'm going to have to try

Step 2:
Write overly dramatic poetry then read it when you want to laugh
and cry at the same time.

As an extra tip: the more metaphors you pack into it, the better

Step 2: Write overly dramatic poetry

So be kind to the brokenhearted
See that they know favor
and grace
Make it so that they may open their wounds
but inflict no more
Be weary of the brokenhearted
they no not how to control their emotion
Emote they will
Cry they will
Feel they will
always
Befriend the brokenhearted
and help them rediscover
the sweet
the bitter
the bitter in the sweet
Allow them to love like they've loved before
and let go of them
never
For they will love you always
with adoration they wish they never had
Entrapped in your rapture
forever the brokenhearted

Step 2: Write overly dramatic poetry

As I lie in bed
My arms outstretched
Even though no one is there
Hoping to feel warmth
Only to find the cold side of the bed
Wondering if it could be you I was reaching for
Or someone I haven't met
But it was someone that doesn't exist
In my dreams they do
But it's not you anymore I reach for

My life is mine now
And even if the cold side of the bed is all I get to feel
It's not half as lonely as it felt to be with you
My life is mine now

Step 2: Write overly dramatic poetry

Why can't I pursue a man
The way that they pursue me?
I'll be called desperate or obsessive
So I have to wait for a man to choose me
Like a flower to be picked out of the ground
No longer belonging to myself but to the man who picked me
But because he picked me, he may put me in water
But I'm bound to die
Because I'm not mine anymore

Step 2: Write overly dramatic poetry

Please listen
Please hear
My cry for help
Hear my tears
They cry for you

Step 2: Write overly dramatic poetry

My life has been falling apart since the day I met you
How can one person cause so much destruction?
How does a termite take down a skyscraper
You ate away my foundation
And once you had taken everything
I crumbled from the inside out
And you left me

To disintegrate

Step 2: Write overly dramatic poetry

A lifetime in two years
Love me forever
Take me with you in your dreams

Step 2: Write overly dramatic poetry

Even though we are apart my love for you still grows daily
I give to you the sacrificial love that my Savior once gave to me
Love is my only gift from God
And I decided a long time ago you should have it
I love you my dear

Step 3:
Pine after anyone and anything

Step 3: Pine after anyone and anything

Covered in the salt of my own skin
I sit up
Alone
Thinking of a time I once had with you
Knowing nothing and no one will ever bring it back
Like a woodpecker in my mind's tree
Chipping away at my memories
Gnawing at my soul
I await
For life's next distraction

I love falling in love
I love everything about it

I love the way that it feels like you're simultaneously lighting every
one of your cells on fire
And creating them all at once
You suddenly know exactly what you're doing
And have no idea when it will all fall from under you

I love when you look at them and see every memory you hope will
come to life
When seeing their face quiets the world around you

Obsession is the most powerful drug

Step 3: Pine after anyone and anything

Let me die at your feet
I want to feel that kind of desperation

Despair is my favorite emotion
When I fall apart it's almost like every part of me is living

Just like abusive men, I crave sadness
Until it's mine

Fall in love with me
And not just because I told you to

Do it because you know you've always felt that way
The night I told you that I loved you
After a year of knowing that I loved you
I used every last ounce of courage
I will ever possess

You shut me down
So for the love of the Lord
Will you just love me back?
For once?

I'm not desperate
I'm just a woman who knows what she wants
And I want it with you

I have all my love
Waiting for your arrival
Please come and take it

Step 3: Pine after anyone and anything

Asking you to love me
Was the single most selfish thing I've ever done
And then I did it again to another
But the single most selfish thing you ever did
Was indulge my request
You told me day after day that you loved me
But you never did
That kills me still
My soul has been dying ever since that happened
You plagued my heart
But I let you

Step 3: Pine after anyone and anything

You're eyes were as black as tar
So gorgeous
That I fell right in
And got stuck

Step 3: Pine after anyone and anything

Holding your hand close to mine
I feel limitless
Into the clouds we wander

Step 3.5:
Write down your most memorable kisses and how they felt

Step 3.5: Write down your most memorable kisses

My first kiss?

We can forget about it
Just like fourteen year old me tried to forget it

What can I say?
When it's not right, it's not right

Thank you for taking me to the mall
And thank you for smelling nice

Step 3.5: Write down your most memorable kisses

My first love rocked my world
Did I understand him?
No
What did I see in him?
He was different
He had that thing about him

That thing that leather jackets have
That thing that loud music has
That thing that jumping in the ocean with all your clothes on has

When we kissed it was like all the stars aligned all at once
Like every thought in my head was clear
Like we weren't in the back of some mall parking lot in the freezing
cold
Like I don't even remember what we were talking about it

But it was important

Step 3.5: Write down your most memorable kisses

Kiss me
Kiss me like that boy who tries to forget that he fell in love with me
The night at that concert that he won free tickets

He asked if I was going
Of course I was

We were sixteen
We were doe-eyed
There's nothing more magical than fleeting moments of young love

He was the best friend
His lips tasted like mint-gum, nervous-flavored betrayal

He held my waist
And kissed me so hard that the world stopped

I forgot ~~my~~ our favorite band was playing

It was his first kiss
And the best I ever had

Step 3.5: Write down your most memorable kisses

The most passionate kiss was a mistake
We both knew as soon as it happened

But it had to happen
It was four years overdue
Sometimes kissing your friends puts things to rest

Even though I never said so
I felt everything you did

Step 3.5: Write down your most memorable kisses

How could I kiss you for hours and yet you felt nothing?
How could you kiss my face and then throw my affection back in
my face?
And how is your face still so kissable?
How could you kiss me like that and not love me?
How could you hold me like that and not love me?
How could you say you never loved me?
How could your actions scream the opposite of your words?

Who are you?

Step 3.5: Write down your most memorable kisses

My happiest kiss
Is each one I shared with you

Your lips taste like home

When I step into your bedroom I'm transported to my happiest
memories
I've suffered the most when I was with you

But your your cute freckles remind me that I'm okay
Your smile
Your glasses
And your dancing

I think maybe my suffering might be over

But your kiss reminds me that I'll never truly be happy
I'll never love anyone like I've loved you
And you'll never love me back

Step 4:
Allow yourself to have earth-shattering existential crises

Step 4: Allow yourself to have earth-shattering existential crises

Oh solitude, my old friend
Oh isolation, my dear enemy
Oh loneliness, my past lover
How I desire to be free
Oh silence, please forgive me
Oh expression, please embrace me
Oh emotion, please have mercy
How I desire to be free
Though loneliness will love me better
Though isolation knows me best
Though solitude comforts me more
How I desire to be free
Though silence gives me clarity
Though expression gives me peace
Though emotion gives me life
How I desire to be free
Oh death, how I crave you
Oh violence, how I seek you
Oh sleep, how I adore you
How I know I will never be free
Though death you are certain
Though violence you are eternal
Though sleep you waste my life
How I desire to be free

Step 4: Allow yourself to have earth-shattering existential crises

Tenía
el miedo de su gente
en sus ojos

Todo va a cambiar
cerca

no sabe qué hacer

Ella no se preparé

Ella me dijo que
"quiero comer el mundo
pero no tengo una boca"

Step 4: Allow yourself to have earth-shattering existential crises

- It's hard to remain hopeful when I remember that things got so bad that I started to write down nice things you had once said to me

- It's hard to remain hopeful when I think about the fact that I can't have a conversation with you without feeling like you're looking through me

- It's hard to remain hopeful when I think about how depressed and lonely I felt after you continued to sleep with me after it was over

- It's hard to remain hopeful when I stay up at night and wonder if any of those memories are real

- It's hard to remain hopeful about anything, really

Birth.

You don't start living until the day you fall in love
But the day your heart is broken is the day you start dying

Death.

How many times can you start a prayer with:

Dear God
I am so broken
I need your strength
I need your guidance
I need more faith in You

before God gets tired of hearing that?

What kind of Christian am I when I'm full of sadness?

Step 4: Allow yourself to have earth-shattering existential crises

Being raped is:

Being a stranger in your own skin
All of your self respect being stripped
Being silenced
Being exposed
Having your body be out of your control
Having someone invade your personal space's personal space
Being forced to relearn radical self love
Craving companionship without the ability to trust
<u>Being betrayed by your own love language</u>
Being a foreigner in your own body
Wanting to ask for help but suddenly no longer able to speak your own language
The moment your body becoming the graveyard for your dreams

Step 4: Allow yourself to have earth-shattering existential crises

When your soul is trapped in a beautiful body
Your skin becomes someone else's sexual playground
The way that people look at you changes as soon as you turn 12
People begin to undress you with their eyes
I wish they wouldn't just peel away my clothes
I with they would peel away my skin
So they might see
That I'm just a soul
Trapped in a flesh and bone vessel

Step 4: Allow yourself to have earth-shattering existential crises

Loneliness is the thief
Who shakes you awake in the night and says:
"You'll never be loved"
"You're going to feel like this forever"

And then proceeds to choke you to the point of death
Just as your face turns blue and you beg him to end it
Loneliness lets go
And you take a long, sharp inhale
The color comes back into your face

Then roll over to the cold side of the bed
Where the absence of a person sets in
Sigh a breath of gratitude for your life
Go back to sleep
And look forward to the next time loneliness visits

Step 4: Allow yourself to have earth-shattering existential crises

I feel despair
In the front of my face
And in the depths of my body

As if my soul turns into chewing gum
And gets stretched in half
Desperately trying not to snap

Just before it relentlessly takes me
Hope turns me back into a person
And prepares my heart to be hurt again

Step 4: Allow yourself to have earth-shattering existential crises

Depression
Hollowed out my insides
And fed them to my fears

Step 4: Allow yourself to have earth-shattering existential crises

When I run from the ocean of Living Water
My lips drip of loneliness
I perspire beads of despair
And I bleed with heartbreak
I do all these things when I return to the Living Ocean
It does not mean I have an absence of these feelings
But they are washed away
My spirit is refreshed
And I can breathe my Father's breath

Step 4: Allow yourself to have earth-shattering existential crises

What I fear most
Is that I've hurt someone
The way that others have hurt me
It kills me to think that there might be someone as heartbroken as I
am
And it was done by mine own hand

If so, I'm sorry
I'm so sorry

Step 4: Allow yourself to have earth-shattering existential crises

The eyes of depression light
As it sees your fears
Burns delight and desire

Step 5:
Reflect on the folks who never loved you back

On that night
the moon shone so brightly
that the ocean glistened in the darkness
She realized
where art thou Romeo?
but he was nowhere to be found

So forget me not
My forbidden love

Step 5: Reflect on the folks who never loved you back

I look at you
And see a future I wish I got to have in your eyes

In your smile
I hear wedding bells that are silenced forever

Your face
Is like a fading dream

Can you be nostalgic for a life you never got to live?

I wonder if you know that no one will ever love you like I will

The day I stop hurting
Is the day I learn that pining can't grow anything

When I plant my own seeds in the gardens of joy
I won't need you anymore

But I'll still wonder
Was it ever us?

"I missed your body"
The words cut deep into me
As if they stabbed me and asked, "did you like that?"
What kind of a thing is that to say to someone?
"I missed your body"

You didn't miss my laugh
- My jokes
- My thought provoking ideas
- My listening skills
- My kindness
- My calm nature

Not even
- My scent
- My warmth
- My touch
- My kiss

You missed my body
It's like I presented you the most important gift of myself
And all you wanted was the wrapping paper

Next time
Miss something else beside my body
Miss something better

Tenés el infierno de mi corazón en
Vos ojos
Cuando me viste
Temo
No querés mi corazón
Querés mi cerebro
Pero mi cerebro es mío
Mi corazón es tuyo
Tenés el corazón de vos mamá
Y el encantador de vos papá
Y los ojos del diablo
Es una combinación fatalidad
Pero
Cuando estoy libre de vos
Vuelo
Temo no sea posible
Temo para mi corazón

Step 5: Reflect on the folks who never loved you back

I see you around a lot
And you smile a friendly smile
Like you've already forgotten what you did to me
The psychological torment
The depression we went through
The bickering
The trash talking

You smile like none of it happened
I still remember
And hopefully
By the time I have finished this book
It will be cathartic enough
To allow me to never think about you again

And then maybe I'll be able to return the forgetful, apathetic smile
that looks so nice on you

Step 5: Reflect on the folks who never loved you back

I know that I have known true love
Even if I never meet anyone else
Even if you never saw the value in me
I so love you
And I'll die carrying this love for you in my heart
But I love you enough now
To let you go
I can die knowing that you had my heart
And got to keep it
It was all worth it
It was all worth it for you

Step 5: Reflect on the folks who never loved you back

I hope that in a parallel universe
You really loved me
Or that maybe we're in someone else's simulation
And that they know that you love me
But you didn't have the guts to say so
Or maybe you don't
Maybe you never did
I wasn't a hopeless romantic before I met you
I didn't even like poetry before I met you
Now that you've turned my whole world upside down
You're gone

Step 5: Reflect on the folks who never loved you back

One day I will cease to breathe
My heart will cease to beat
And my soul will still flutter
At the sound of your name

Step 6:
Learning how to live when your broken heart won't stop beating

Self love.
Time.
Forgiveness.

Those things, in that order are the only way to fill your hole. It's the only thing that will ever make you whole.

Love is my addiction
it's the drug that I'm willing to fight for
it's the bad one
Jesus even told us that
as Christians
we can have faith
we can be steadfast
we can uphold all the commandments
but without Love
we have nothing
we must Love God with all our heart, soul, and mind
and Love our neighbors
but we must also Love ourselves
for we cannot Love ourselves without loving God
for we cannot Love others without loving ourselves
Love is worth compromising everything for
when they ask whatever happened to me
tell them
Love can have me
I am ready to be swallowed whole
chewed up
and spit out
all over again

Love be my beautiful demise

Always be the student of tragedy
Your worst emotions
are your best teachers

Step 6: Learning how to live when your broken heart won't stop beating

When you find out that giving your life to God gives you purpose
and not happiness;
You begin to learn what you're really in for
Your purpose could include some suffering
I'll save you the trouble: there's going to be suffering
God is softening your heart for something greater
There is power in your suffering

Finding Christ doesn't mean you're happy
Because I have deep joy
And deep sadness

I want to pick a man up
Buy him dinner
Show him a good time
Make the first move
And kiss him
But I can't
Because while my feminine identity is rooted so deep that it has
blossomed into a tall, gorgeous willow
Masculinity is a house of cards
One blow to the ego and the whole structure falls apart and
crushes a man's self worth

That's why I don't like courting or dating
I guess I could never really buy into heterosexuality
Because it was never entirely made for me

As sun turns to night
And moonlight is shown
My true sadness comes out
She's ready to go home

Home from this body
Home from this soul
My authenticity flourishes
From my decaying soul

Sadness is here
She's here to stay
She's part of who I am
And maybe I like it that way

Let the tears fall
Out of your eyes
Let them flow like a river
Carving a new life for you
May they be the path you float down
To hope
To learning
To self love
Let them flow like a river
Out of your heart
Into the light
Allow the vulnerability to wash over you
Like taking a bath with truth
You will come out
With the clarity of clean eyes
And a free heart

The spiral is the heart's desired shape
It tumbles and twists
Carries you to the depth of emotion
Cycles you through
In life and death
Your heart's fire is eternal
Spiraling into the nothingness
Beating around pain and love
Thumping inside an empty chest
Waiting to be returned
To the arms of my lover

My body is like butter
But my personality is like sandpaper
I have learned to love both
But the lovers in my life could not

I'm still waiting for the one
Who is both an unfinished table
And a slice of toast
So that I may both fulfill my duty
And find a use for this body and soul

Step 6: Learning how to live when your broken heart won't stop beating

Remember something:
A broken heart
Beats for two

Step 6: Learning how to live when your broken heart won't stop beating

I won't ever go back to you
The arms of my Savior are so much sweeter
And have never once abandoned me

I am *worthy* of so much more

I looked into a telescope
And saw my future
I saw stars
And I saw God's unfailing love
And I didn't see you

And I was okay

Step 6: Learning how to live when your broken heart won't stop beating

Eyes lit up like lightbulbs
To see clouds flying by
Eyes for which I could see the grassy meadows
Green so green it stung my eyes
The vibrance of spring upon me

Seeing the world as if it were the first time
My broken heart gave me two new eyes
Clear and bright after the rain of tears
As the warmth of the first sunny day of March melted my frozen
body
I could see a new future beyond my own horizon

The day my broken heart stopped bleeding
The day my broken heart kept beating

Step 7:
Write letters of forgiveness

To The One I'll Never Understand,

Thank you for making me so happy.
Even with all the garbage we put each other through, I still think
that we're very compatible. I think that if we had met in different
circumstances, better places in our mental health, and further
along in our faith journeys, we could have made things work.
I want you to know how much I loved you. I was so in love with
you that I feared that I will never love someone that much ever
again. And even though you said you never felt that way about me,
deep down, I think you did. Maybe that's just the hopeless
romantic in me.
You really made an effort to know me and it was a pleasure to
know you. I wish you had put in as much effort into loving me as
you put into knowing me.
I was really happy when I was with you.
I remember when you came to visit me and I showed you where I
worked, you gave me a piggyback ride. You spun me around so fast
that I couldn't walk straight. I was so happy that day that I'm
crying as I write this.
I want you to know that this isn't some sappy love letter that I'm
writing out of emotion, I've thought about writing this for a long
time. However, you have a history of not reading my letters, so I
figured I wouldn't give this one to you.
I wish I could tell you that loving someone is the greatest and
scariest thing you'll ever do. It hurts and it's a risk but that's why it's
worth it.
I wish I could tell you that if you stopped treating life like cost-
benefit analysis, you would be much happier.
I wish I could tell you that looking at your face gives me a rush of
uncontrollable memories and emotions from a time I will never get
back and that's why I can't be around you.

I wish I could shake the way I notice you when you pass by. And I wish you didn't have the power to flatten me with your words.
I wish I could tell you that when you spoke, I really listened. Here are some things that you said that I still think about:
The golden rule is bullshit: You should treat people as they want to be treated and not how you want to be treated
You made an effort to control all of your body movement in order to be more efficient - I've never met anyone with that much bodily discipline
When you switched from saying "I love you" to "thank you" as a response when I told you I loved you
Asking someone to love you is unfair but it doesn't mean that all of the rage and despair that I felt wasn't valid.
I only want joy and peace for you. Remember that you can't control anything in life, especially the people around you.
If you ever read this, do me a favor and call me when you meet the love of your life. I want to know how amazing she is. I want to know that you're happy. I want to know that you will love someone the way that I loved you.

Signed: Emma

To My Most Beloved,

I am going to dance with you at your wedding and wish it was me
you were marrying. I'm going to die wishing that I could have
spent my life with you. I am only twenty years old and I already
know that you are my only regret in life.
How was I so lucky to have you in my life for two years?
How was I so unlucky to have met the single most wonderful thing
in my life and watch it slip away.
I love you so much that if I died tomorrow, I would die knowing
that I had a soulmate.
You're everything I've ever wanted.
You've been so loving and caring and kind, I think how could I
deserve such a man?
But I didn't.
But I love you enough to let you go.
I'm excited to watch you find love and to be truly happy.
I'm excited to see you create a family.
Know that I will be watching your life unfold with joy.
Know that through a glass window, I will watch my life pass by.
A life with you was the only hope that was getting me by.
A life that someone else will get to have with you.
A life I will simply watch from afar.

It wasn't until you that I realized that you can die of a broken
heart.
But it's much worse to survive.

Signed: Emma

Dearest Depression,

I hope one day to greet you as an old friend.
For now you are my abusive ex-husband who won't get out of my house.
Your presence is a reminder of all of the loss and heartache I have suffered.
I'm just grateful you're letting me feel my emotions again.
Remember that summer we spent together? It was just you and I back then. I cried so much that summer begging to feel something beside your all consuming emptiness. Thank you for forcing me to look at all of the other demons that were living inside of me.
You have been a worthy adversary in my life.
But please, please, let me go.
Move out of my house, get a career, and get a new apartment.
Please don't leave your furniture.
I'm tired of all the fighting.
I just want to go a day without your nagging.
Once you move out, I promise to process our long and tumultuous relationship. I will look back on the good lessons I have learned when we lived together.
And then I will greet you as an old friend.

Signed: Emma

To My Abusers,

You don't remember me. But I remember you.
What you did to me was not okay. Nothing will take away what you did to me. But I have great compassion for you.
I was not a victim or a survivor of what you did because I choose for my experiences not to be part of my identity.
I did not report you because I was ashamed, I blamed myself. I had a hard time defining what happened that day as abuse.
I have compassion for you because I believe that forgiveness is the only way for things to get better.
You didn't have anything to prove to me.
Yet you hurt me anyway.
I'm sorry you were hurting.
You don't have to hurt anymore, but what you need to do is man up.
Manning up means that you take responsibility for your actions, starting with taking responsibility for hurting me.
Feel your emotions, ground your emotions. Allow them to come and pass.
When you feel like giving up and succumbing to your emotions, rely on your friends.
When you feel despair and depression, remember that your actions made me feel those two emotions everyday for the last six years of my life.
Remember it doesn't get easier but it becomes tolerable.
And then forgive yourself.
You can be better, you are not a bad person. You just needed compassion.

Signed: A Stranger

Dear Emma,

I forgive you.
I forgive you for not always having the energy to fight for what you
believe. I forgive you for all of the countless mistakes you make
over and over again. I forgive you for allowing yourself to fall in
love with people who were never going to love you. I forgive you for
flirting with depression, hanging out with anxiety, and wasting your
life away pining after despair.
I love you so much.
And I'm trying to do right by you. I surrendered myself to God
and that means we don't have to walk alone anymore. Everyday
I'm getting better and becoming a better person. I don't know how
much time I will get to spend on earth hanging out with you but, so
far, I've had an amazing time with you.
You're fearless and bold and kind.
Never forget where you've walked and take some time to reflect on
how far you've come.
You're journey with me has been my favorite. I will always love you
and do my best to care for you from now until the day it's time to
leave.

Love: Self

To the Reader

I've wanted to write a book for as long as I can remember and this is just the beginning of something great. Thank you for listening. Listening is what this world is deeply lacking and it's something that I work toward everyday. We have so much more to learn from one another.

Your story is the most powerful thing that you own. Don't let anyone else write it except for you. You are in control of your story so; make it good.

Most lovingly,
E. P. Johnson

P.S. I will write you again soon.